THE MULLET REPORT

THE MULLET REPORT

MULLETS ARE GREAT AGAIN!

RONALD REDAKTOR

SKYHORSE PUBLISHING

Skyhorse Publishing books may be purchased in bulk at special discounts for sales promotion, corporate gifts, fund-raising, or educational purposes. Special editions can also be created to specifications. For details, contact the Special Sales Department, Skyhorse Publishing, 307 West 36th Street, 11th Floor, New York, NY 10018 or info@skyhorsepublishing.com.

Skyhorse® and Skyhorse Publishing® are registered trademarks of Skyhorse Publishing, Inc.®, a Delaware corporation.

Visit our website at www.skyhorsepublishing.com.

10 9 8 7 6 5 4 3 2 1

Library of Congress Cataloging-in-Publication Data is available on file.

Cover design by Brian Peterson.

Print ISBN: 978-1-5107-5365-5
Ebook ISBN: 978-1-5107-5366-2

Printed in the United States of America

VOLUME I

Volume I
I. The Special Hair Investigation

"I hope they now go and take a look at the oranges. The oranges of the, uh, uh, investigation."

Discussing the Mueller Investigation, April 2, 2019

Volume I
II. #MulletStyle Social Media Campaign

"My hair may not be perfect, but it's mine."

Twitter, April 24, 2013

Volume I
III. Hair Hacking and Dumping Operations

"No animals have been harmed in the creation of my hairstyle."

How to Get Rich, Donald Trump

Volume I
IV. Brushin' Collusion in the #MulletStyle Campaign

"I will never change this hairstyle, I like it. It fits my head.

Harm to Ongoing Matter

Do you want to touch it?"

Volume I
V. Prosecution and Declination Decisions

"I've said if Ivanka weren't my daughter, perhaps I'd be dating her . . ."

The View, March 6, 2006

VOLUME II

Volume II
I. Background Hair and Beauty Principles

"I get up, take a shower, and wash my hair. Then I read the newspapers and watch the news on television, and slowly the hair dries. It takes about an hour. I don't use the blow dryer. Once it's dry I comb it."

Playboy, March 1, 1990

"I will also admit that I color my hair. Somehow the color never looks great, but what the hell, I just don't like gray hair."

How to Get Rich, Donald Trump

Volume II
II. Factual Results of the Hair Investigation

"As everybody knows, but the haters and losers refuse to acknowledge, I do not wear a 'wig.'"

Twitter, April 24, 2013

Volume II
III. Legal Defenses to the Application of Hair Products

"Once I have it the way I like it—even though nobody else likes it—I spray it, and it's good for the day."

Playboy, March 1, 1990

Volume II
IV. Conclusion

"The Mueller Witch Hunt is completely OVER!"

Twitter, May 1, 2019